Dedicated to Peg and Ed.

Andreas Mueller

Markus Hoevener

International SEO – Plotting the Course

A Compact Guide:

Domain Strategies, Markup Tips, Linking Advice, Hreflang Implementations, Best-of-breed Tools & More

This succinct, step-by-step Playbook will empower you to navigate the perplexing & treacherous waters of International Optimization, giving you access to new and unchartered Global Markets.

Table of Contents

1. So Why this Book?

I have been involved in optimization since the very early days going back over 15 years. Markus Hoevener and I started up Bloofusion when most people hadn't heard of SEO and Google had just stepped on the search engine stage to compete with the likes of Lycos, Yahoo and Alta Vista. Having worked with various companies it has become clear that, although most of our projects are fairly customized, there are certain core challenges and questions that resurface again and again.

Hence the idea for this book. One of the topics that almost always will enter the discussion is *International SEO*. And although currently there are countless technical features that enable international SEO, such as the *hreflang tag*, very few companies, even among the Fortune 500 list, take advantage of these tags. We were both taken aback.

There is an immense need for guidance in this field. The book you hold in your hands tries to outline and resolve the issues surrounding the internationalization of SEO and provides a playbook for you to base your decisions upon.

- Which tags can help me support my internationalization efforts most effectively?
- What should a solid domain strategy look like for my online presence?
- And which tools are available to achieve that?

You will find answers to these and more questions on the following pages. If you think I have missed a point or even two, please send me an email at seobook@bloofusion.com and I'll be happy to cover that in the next edition.

2. What about International SEO?

Although the US trade deficit is on everybody's minds, in terms of sheer volume, our country is still toward the top of the list of global exporters, beating both Germany and Japan. And just as important as it is to export products into other countries, a website needs to consider exporting itself as well. Content needs to not only be translated properly; it must also be optimized for search as well. International search.

International SEO defines all measures and activities that help us achieve this task. Basically we are talking about the following two goals

1. **Appropriate Content Delivery**: Every user should receive the content that is best suited for her country and language. Pricing needs to be localized, the contact info absolutely needs to show local phone numbers and addresses. Legal requirements for this differ in each country. In order to mitigate any losses in lead conversions or sales, the user should always be served the right content.

2. **Optimal Collaboration of Web Properties**: If there are multiple websites, such as website.com, website.de, website.fr or website sections, such as website.com/en/, website.com/de/ or website.com/fr/ it is vital that they all benefit from each other. This means that even though some of your international divisions may not work together or share knowledge seamlessly, on the website everything needs to come together as a whole to display strong leadership and support the smaller country players.

By the way, *international* always sounds like a big deal. It means you are a global player. But it also means that if you're a US company and are covering the Canadian market, this is also is considered international. And thinking strategically about how to deal with the international aspects of SEO becomes vital in this case as well.

On the following pages you will find out how to use some of the technical aids, such as the hreflang tag most effectively. This will enable your site's content to appear in local search results as naturally as possible. Another vital arrow in your quiver of international SEO that will be covered is a well-planned domain strategy.

3. Concepts You Need to Know

Property

Login access to Google Search Console (formerly known as Google Webmaster Tools https://www.google.com/webmasters/tools/) will be required at a few spots to modify settings or verify data. It isn't generally well known that your website can be set up and defined not only once but multiple times. Let me explain…

If your website (www.mysite.com) has two international subdirectories (www.mywebsite.com/en/ for the English content and www.mywebsite.com/fr for the French content) and a subdomain (blog.mywebsite.com), then these can be entered as separate **properties**. The benefit is that you can easily manage global settings for each of these directories, i.e. you can establish that all content within www.mywebsite.com/fr (French content) is aligned with a specific country (in this case France). But more about this later.

Variants

In this book I will refer to variants. What is meant here is web pages with the same content. This content, however, is provided either in different languages or for different countries.

Let me illustrate this point with an example:

The page http://www.mywebsite.com/page is a page in English

The German translation of the content will be found here http://www.mywebsite.com/seite (*Seite* means *page* in German)

Both of these pages are **variants**. Same content, simply the language is different.

Directories & Subdomains

There are various approaches to setting up international web structures or their URLs. Of course, there is the traditional approach such as appending a "?lang=de" to the URL. But best to avoid these sorts of awkward solutions since they have been replaced by more effective measures.

Two better avenues to take are the following. They will also be covered in sufficient detail later on in this book.

1. **Directories**: All content is located in directories, which are displayed in the URL path. Typically, this is done directly in the top-level directory i.e. www.mywebsite.com/de/ for German pages and www.mywebsite.com/fr/ for French pages.

2. **Subdomains**: Even though the term *subdomain* is actually incorrect, its usage has become widespread. What is meant here is that the language or country is included as part of the domain. For example: de.mywebsite.com for all German content and fr.mywebsite.com for all French content.

Which of these options is better suited for your needs depends on your individual case and I will delve into this more as we progress.

4. Domain Strategy

What is the point?

When choosing a domain strategy, it is vital to determine the domains under which the individual countries or languages should be organized. There are two primary paths to take here:

1. Use a **country-specific domain** for each country (ccTLD – country-code top-level domain). So if you are active in the US, France and Spain, you would use these three domains:

   www.mywebsite.us (but generally www.mywebsite.com)

   www.mywebsite.fr

   www.mywebsite.es

2. Use a gTLD, a **generic top-level domain** (.com, .net, .info). The individual country or language versions are then implemented as directories (eg www.mywebsite.com/fr for French content) or as a subdomain (fr.mywebsite.com).

In practice there may be mixing and matching such as using separate local domains (www.mywebsite.de and www.mywebsite.fr) for the most important markets and for the less important territories a more generic domain, (i.e. www.mywebsite.com/ru/ for Russian content).

ccTLDs – Blessing or Curse?

One point should be made clear beyond any doubt: There is a massive advantage if you use country-specific domains (ccTLDs) – they work very well within that country. So, if you already have a .de domain, you'll find that it produces top results within Germany.

For other countries this domain will not work so reliably – primarily because it is not likely to be clicked on by users in search results. If you want to buy a product in France and see a .es domain (Spain) in the search results, you will be less likely to click on such a search result compared to a local .fr domain. This is because you intuitively have certain expectations and you may perceive a certain level of risk: How is the delivery time when I order something from Spain? How is customer service? Will they understand me when I speak French? What is the legal situation for certain products?

With a local domain, you are 100% committed to a specific country. It makes little sense to integrate other country or language versions within a country-specific domain. So if you only have one domain in Europe such as www.mywebsite.de and then create folders for other European countries (i.e. www.mywebsite.de/ru/ for Russian content), this will usually produce worse results than with a country-specific domain (www.mywebsite.ru).

If you think that we have now fully addressed the language issue with the best solution being the country-specific domains option – that's not necessarily the case. The equation isn't quite so simple. But stay tuned. We'll get you through the weeds.

Aspect #1: External Linking

Coming from the Google perspective, it is no secret that a website is also heavily judged by its external linking. This means, the more external sites with thematically appropriate content you can get linking back to your own site, the better your ranking will be.

Let's take a look at a concrete example here: the automobile manufacturer Audi. They own the following list of country domains. The domain popularity indicates how many external referring domains point back to each of the individual country sites.

Domain	Domain Popularity
www.audi.com	7,700
www.audi.de	6,000
www.audi.co.uk	2,100
www.audi.fr	911
www.audi.ru	830
www.audi.nl	669
www.audi.at	534
www.audi.com.au	514
www.audi.pl	362
www.audi.sk	141
www.audi.is	11

This is actually quite a typical picture: The main or US site (.com) has links from 7,700 different external websites while the Icelandic site (.is) only has 11 inbound links. Depending on how competitive the queries are, this Icelandic site will have a much tougher time appearing at the top for relevant searches. Similarly for countries like Slovakia (.sk) and Poland (.pl).

If we recall the two domain strategies covered previously, the following will apply for Audi:

1. If you utilize multiple country domains, it must be clear that each domain is a solo fighter. The German .de domain has a link popularity of 6,000 but the Icelandic domain doesn't benefit from those links in the least.

2. If you place your bets on a common domain, then you're basically investing into one and the same account. This is especially true when using directories. One good link to www.mywebsite.com/en/ strengthens the domain www.mywebsite.com and subsequently all of the other variants, i.e. www.mywebsite.com/de and www.mywebsite.com/is. For subdomains, this trickle down effect is not as pronounced. So, if an external site links to de.mywebsite.com this link will primarily benefit this specific subdomain. Some of the link power will be shared with the other subdomains, such as fr.mywebsite.com but to a much lesser extent than if you were to use the directory model.

When you're deciding on a strategy, you need to consider whether enough external links can be created for the respective country websites. In reality it often is the case for smaller markets that only a minimal number of employees are on the ground. So it will be quite a challenge to find team members who have the time, are internet savvy and motivated enough to drive the massive effort of a local link campaign.

Aspect #2: Ratings and reviews

Another vital point to consider is the accumulation of ratings by Google. In Google ads you will frequently see the so-called Seller Rating Extensions (https://support.google.com/adwords/answer/2375474?hl=en)

Surf Equipment Rental Santa Cruz, CA - Club Ed - Club Ed Surf School
https://club-ed.com/surf-equipment-rental/ ▾
★★★★★ Rating: 5 - 24 reviews
Surf Equipment Rentals (Included Free with Lessons) ... Our surf equipment rentals are located on Cowell Beach, to the right hand side of the wharf. Look for our Blue "Learn to Surf" trailer on the beach in front of the Dream Inn Hotel.

Illustration 1: This organic result for *wet suit rental* indicates accumulated ratings

Google compiles these ratings from various platforms (Trusted Shops, eKomi, TRUSTPILOT & others) und ends up generating a single overall rating. This rating is based on each subdomain.

Depending on your strategy, the rating will be calculated in different ways:

Domain Strategy	Calculation of Rating
Every country has its **own domain**, such as .de, .fr, etc.	Every country receives its own rating. I.e. one for .de, one for .fr, etc.
There is an overarching, **generic domain with directories**, such as .com/de/, .com/fr/, .com/es/ etc.	The ratings of all of these countries are added up.
There is an overarching, **generic domain with subdomains**, such as de.mywebsite.com, fr.mywebsite.com ...	Every subdomain receives its own rating. I.e. one for de., one for fr., etc.

You also should be aware that the ratings stars will only be visible if at least 30 reviews have been submitted in the last 12 months. And their cumulative rating must be at least 3.5 out of 5 stars.

In terms of your domain strategy you need to think about the following considerations:

> If you prefer having your own domain or subdomain for each country, you will discover that in weak markets you may not be able to collect the necessary number of reviews. In that case it would be advantageous to use a generic overall domain, such as .com, so that you would accumulate stars in these smaller markets.

> If you have one country with high ratings and another one with especially low ones, you may actually want to avoid paying all of these ratings into the same account. The lower ratings in one market will influence the higher ones in the other and end up reducing your stars overall.

> You can view the actual reviews by clicking on the *rating* link in an Adwords ad like this:

Top 5 Bluetooth Headsets
[Ad] www.bestreviews.com/Bluetooth-Headsets ▾
4.9 ★★★★★ rating for bestreviews.com
We Analyzed Every Bluetooth Headset Our Top Pick Will Surprise You!
"The Modern-Day Version of Consumer Reports" – Huffington Post
Best Bang for Your Buck · Best of the Best · View our Top Products · How We Test

Also consider that if all international reviews are flowing into the same account, you may see foreign reviews that don't make sense in your local language. This could confuse a visitor and possibly discourage them from making a purchase. Just wanted to point that out.

Aspect #3: Bad Links

In the past, companies have used various strategies to build inbound links to a website, unfortunately many of these were in direct violation of Google's guidelines. Through updates like Google Penguin, Google is in a position to fairly easily sniff out bad links, i.e. massive linking schemes via blog comments. This can lead to minor or even substantial penalties for your rankings.

If you use a generic domain, there is a potential risk that bad links for a country could affect the entire site. So if the local online marketing manager for Russia purchases bad links pointing to his directory www.mywebsite.com/ru/, these links would not only damage the /ru directory, but the entire domain would be affected, i.e. all directories under www.mywebsite.com.

It is, therefore, extremely important to keep an eye on external links and give clear guidance to the local country teams who are focused on these. This means: no purchasing of links, no link exchanges, no registrations with inferior directories. As painful as it may sound, you need to stay away from activities that promise maximum benefits with minimal effort. There just is no free lunch.

Aspect #4: Agility

The topic of agility is not typically an SEO topic – yet it plays a significant role in practice. For international companies it often makes sense to have a website setup, where the structure is identical in all countries and for all languages. The main content is localized, i.e. translated and possibly adapted locally to each market.

This may be practical and useful. It definitely helps the smaller countries still have attractive content, for example, even though their web staff may not possess the same resources and motivation to publish as much. Unfortunately, this also means that your site content isn't particularly agile. In this case it's not possible to create a blog entry for only one country, even if it might be very applicable. And any changes to the content have to first be discussed with the local author in charge.

It may make sense to sacrifice agility for function and efficiency. In the case of a generic domain, most companies opt for the *translate + adapt* approach, so that should be consider in your overall domain strategy.

Aspect #5: Local Color

I have already touched upon this aspect and it's definitely worth putting a lot of consideration into it. Here's why...

Imagine you are a local British prospect and search for *percussion shops* on Google UK. Would you be tempted to click on the second result? This is clearly a website hosted in Germany with a .de domain.

Buy drums and other percussion instruments online ...
https://auctionata.com/intl/**shop**/musical.../**percussive**-instruments ▾
Old and well-maintained European and international percussive instruments ■
Originally painted tambourines and small drums from the 1930s and 1950s.

Welcome - Thomann UK
www.thomann.de/gb/index.html ▾
www.thomann.de - The Online Shop of Europe's Biggest Retailer of Musical Equipment
... Guitars and Basses · Drums and Percussion Drums + Percussion ...

Percussion - Sundown Guitars Online Shop (Powered by ...
www.sundownguitars.co.uk/**shop/percussion**/cat_48.html ▾
Sundown Guitars Online Shop. A full range of Electric, Acoustic & Bass Guitars and Accessories.

Illustration 2: A German (.de) result appearing in a UK (.co.uk) search.

Even though I haven't found any reliable studies substantiating this: Basically, I assume that users prefer to click on their *own* local domains and rarely on local domains of other countries. For a generic domain, I think the problem is not so serious because many users are much more accustomed to clicking on a .com or .org result.

Even if thomann.de (see illustration above) is very successful with its online business in the German market: I personally would never choose a country-specific domain strategy to build local presences.

Implementing your Strategy

Whichever path you take, there is a lot to be considered after your strategy has been defined and finalized. If you are starting out from scratch with a new website, you may want to skip this section. But with most websites there has been a previous life with potential issues and they must be considered and dealt with.

If you want to make changes to your domain or URL structure, it is absolutely vital to use **301 redirects** to redirect the old URLs to the new ones. So if you previously had a country-specific domain for France and thus a URL like www.mywebsite.fr/page.html and starting today you opted to put everything on a generic .com domain, then this page will be reachable via the new URL www.mywebsite.com/fr/page.html. You now will need to set up a 301 (permanent) redirect from the original page. Ask your administrator, your IT team or the web agency to do that for you.

If the actual domain is changing, you can also take advantage of Google Search Console to solidify this modification. Under *Settings*, there is the option *Change of Address*, where you can inform Google that the domain will change once you have set up the 301 redirects. Although the 301 redirects that you have already set up should be sufficient, it is good practice to advertise your intentions clearly to Google within Search Console.

Illustration 3: Domain changes should be clearly communicated via Google Search Console

5. Integrating the hreflang Tag

What does the tag look like?

The hreflang tag is a relatively simple tag that gets placed in the <head> section of a website and looks like this:

```
<link rel="alternate" hreflang="Language" href="URL" />
```

A concrete example would be:

```
<link rel="alternate" hreflang="de"
href="http://www.mywebsite.com/page/" />
```

The language specific in the attribute *hreflang* is a two-letter code defined by the norm ISO 639-1. A list of all codes (de for German, en for English, etc.) can be found on this page http://en.wikipedia.org/wiki/List_of_ISO_639-1_codes.

Alternatively, a combination of language and country can be specified instead of just language (separated by a hyphen). The country is formed by two letters - according to the standard ISO 3166-1 alpha-2. On the following page, http://en.wikipedia.org/wiki/ISO_3166-1_alpha-2, you can locate all country codes such as *DE* for Germany and *DK* for Denmark, etc.

If you want to define the hreflang tag for the German language and the country Germany it would look like this:

```
<link rel="alternate" hreflang="de-DE"
href="http://www.mywebsite.com/page/" />
```

This tag indicates that the page defined in "href" (in this case http://www.mywebsite.com/page/) is appropriate for German-speaking users in the country Germany.

To use a single tag like this is fairly useless. But once a page possesses several variations of different languages or countries then this hreflang tag becomes much more beneficial.

Let's focus on the two example pages: http://www.mywebsite.com/seite/ (the German page – again, *Seite* in German means *page*) and http://www.mywebsite.com/page/ (the English page) then both of these tags must be installed on each of the pages:

```
<link rel="alternate" hreflang="de"
href="http://www.mywebsite.com/seite/" />

<link rel="alternate" hreflang="en"
href="http://www.mywebsite.com/page/" />
```

At first glance it may seem redundant to have both tags installed on both pages, but it is absolutely necessary in terms of the so-called **self-referencing attribute**. All variants of the page must contain exactly the same self-referencing hreflang tags and refer back to each other.

One thing becomes obvious here: You can either target a page with a language or a combination of language *and* country - but not *only* a country. This is an unfortunate limitation but it doesn't represent a hurdle in practice. There are other options for targeting countries - but we'll get to that later.

In summary, let me make one more point: The hreflang tag only defines the variants of the specific page in question. So, if you include the hreflang tag on the home pages of a website, this helps only the home pages - but none of the lower pages. The tag should, therefore, appear on all relevant pages. If the tag is only on the home page, it will only affect the home page. But in itself this won't have any potential negative effects.

What will the hreflang tag do for you?

Let's look at our specific example: Assuming an English-speaking user searches for a specific page while in Germany. Let's guess that this user has set the browser language to English. Furthermore, let's assume that Google would logically provide the German page http://www.mywebsite.com/seite/ in the search results (and not the English page http://www.mywebsite.com/page/)

In this case, however, Google will then reference back to the hreflang information when compiling the search results. And according to the hreflang tag settings, the English page (http://www.mywebsite.com/page/) is much better suited for the user, thus the German-language version is dynamically replaced by the English-language page. As a result Google is able to **deliver the best page** by following the hreflang directions.

Please note, however, that the German-speaking page would have appeared in the search results in this example. So, in a sense, the hreflang tag helps to replace a *wrong* page (in terms of language or language + country) with a more appropriate page – within the search results.

Currently the hreflang tag lacks some functionality in swapping out pages, as John Mueller from Google confirmed (https://www.seroundtable.com/google-explains-hreflang-doesnt-help-with-rankings-22195.html):

> „So if you have a website [...] that's targeting furniture and you have a UK website and it doesn't show at all in France for example, then just setting up at the hreflang with completely new pages for France wouldn't change anything because we wouldn't have anything to swap out."

Help Setting up the Tag

At first glance, the hreflang tag can be fairly difficult to understand, especially if you don't deal with HTML code every day. If you want some additional help and don't want to create tags manually, consider using a tool like the *hreflang Tags Generator Tool* (http://www.aleydasolis.com/en/international-seo-tools/hreflang-tags-generator/).

For each page in question you have to enter each of the respective variants. So you would start with the English-language page http://www.mywebsite.com/page/ and then click on *+ Add an additional language / country URL version*.

Illustration 4: Selecting country/language in the hreflang Tags Generator Tool.

There you can define the variants for your target page (http://www.mywebsite.com/page/):

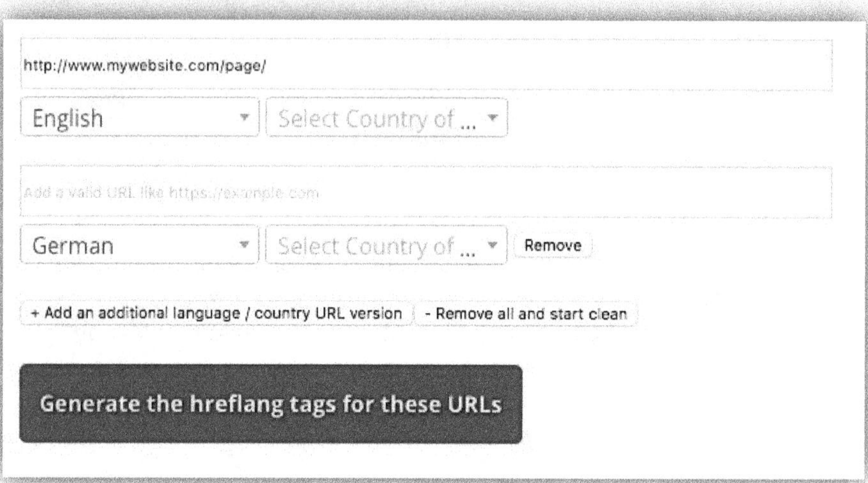

Illustration 5: Each page gets defined.

As soon as all variants are defined, click on the *Generate the hreflang tags for these URLs* and you can copy and paste your code.

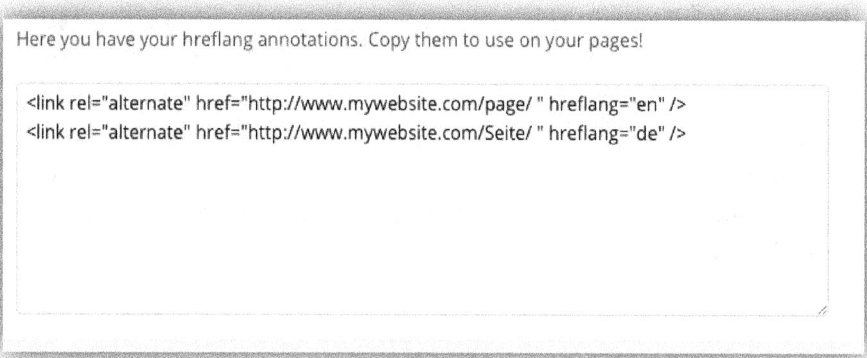

Illustration 6: Your ready-to-use HTML code generated by the hreflang Tags Generator Tool.

Example 1: Canada

Let's say your company is active in Canada, a country where two languages are spoken (English and French). If you have a bilingual website with www.mywebsite.com/en/ for the English side and www.mywebsite.com/fr/ for the French content, then the following hreflang tags should be integrated into the home pages:

```
<link rel="alternate" href="http://www.mywebsite.com/en/" hreflang="en-ca" />

<link rel="alternate" href="http://www.mywebsite.com/nl/" hreflang="fr-ca" />
```

En-ca for English (language) in Canada (country) and fr-ca for French (language) in Canada (country). Both of these tags need to be installed on each of these pages:

http://www.mywebsite.com/en/ and

http://www.mywebsite.com/fr/ and, as already mentioned, for all of the sub-pages in both directories you will also need to set up the appropriate hreflang tags.

Example 2: Belgium

The model is very similar for Belgium, a bilingual country that speaks French and Dutch. The two variants would look like this:

www.mywebsite.com/fr/ for the French-speaking site and

www.mywebsite.com/nl/ for the Dutch version. Here are the hreflang tags to be set up:

```
<link rel="alternate" href="http://www.mywebsite.com/fr/" hreflang="fr-be" />

<link rel="alternate" href="http://www.mywebsite.com/nl/" hreflang="nl-be" />
```

Again: fr-be stands for the French language market within the country of Belgium and nl-be denotes the Dutch language visitors in Belgium.

Both of these tags would need to appear on both pages, i.e. http://www.mywebsite.com/fr/ and http://www.myewebsite.com/nl/ as well as their sub-pages.

Another option would be to select the following hreflang tag:

```
    <link rel="alternate" href="http://www.mywebsite.com/fr/" hre-
flang="fr" />
    <link rel="alternate" href="http://www.mywebsite.com/nl/" hre-
flang="nl" />
```

Why do that instead? Because by using the more specific hreflang tags "fr-be" and "nl-be", you can help Google direct the visitors to the correct pages within Belgium. However, if the visitor is actually located the Netherlands (Dutch), Google would not know which page should be presented. The tag above would address that.

In this case the choice of the hreflang tags also depends on the overall site strategy. If you do not expect visitors from the Netherlands, you can specify the country in the tag – and narrow things down that way. If visitors from the Netherlands are to be driven to the site and you do not have your own content for this country, it would make sense to omit the country specification.

Example 3: DACH

The term DACH (D-Germany , A-Austria, CH-Switzerland) refers to a common European market place. Let's assume a company has a website for Germany (www.mysite.de) and one for the German-speaking visitors in Switzerland (www.mysite.ch).

You could now use hreflang tags in the following manner:

```
<link rel="alternate" href="http://www.mywebsite.de/" hreflang="de-de" />

<link rel="alternate" href="http://www.mywebsite.ch/" hreflang="de-ch" />
```

This approach would easily guide the German-speaking visitors from Germany and Switzerland to the appropriate pages. But what about the German speakers from Austria? If they are to be rerouted to the German .de domain, then choose the following hreflang tags:

```
<link rel="alternate" href="http://www.mywebsite.de/" hreflang="de" />

<link rel="alternate" href="http://www.mywebsite.ch/" hreflang="de-ch" />
```

To make a long story short: Any German speaking visitors from Germany or Austria would end up at the German website (since there is no Austian .at site) and the German speakers from Switzerland would be ushered to the Swiss (.ch) website. All is good.

Alternatives to an HTML tag

As the following two sections will show, the hreflang tag does not necessarily have to be placed in the HTML code. Instead, you can also use XML sitemaps or the HTTP header. This could be relevant for a few special cases, i.e. to define hreflang tags for non-HTML content (for example, PDF files).

But you have to understand that Google can parse this information but many tools do not cope well with it. Debugging is made much more difficult, especially with the use of an XML sitemap, since you cannot just glance at the page to see if the tag is correct.

Alternative Option #1: XML-Sitemap

Over the last few years, Google has defined more and more ways to use XML sitemaps to provide enhanced information. This means that now hreflang information can be delivered to Google via XML sitemaps (https://support.google.com/webmasters/answer/2620865?hl=en).

```xml
<?xml version="1.0" encoding="UTF-8"?>
<urlset xmlns="http://www.sitemaps.org/schemas/sitemap/0.9"
 xmlns:xhtml="http://www.w3.org/1999/xhtml">
 <url>
   <loc>http://www.mywebsite.com/page/</loc>
   <xhtml:link rel="alternate" hreflang="en"
   href="http://www.mywebsite.com/page/" />
   <xhtml:link rel="alternate" hreflang="de"
   href="http://www.mywebsite.com/seite/" />
 </url>

 <url>
   <loc>http://www.mywebsite.com/page/</loc>
   <xhtml:link rel="alternate" hreflang="en"
   href="http://www.mywebsite.com/page/" />
   <xhtml:link rel="alternate" hreflang="en"
   href="http://www.mywebsite.com/seite/" />
 </url>

</urlset>
```

Thus, if there are two pages http://www.mywebsite.com/page/ (EN) and http://www.mywebsite.com/seite/ (DE), the Sitemap must include the following:

1. One block each of the form:

   <Url> <loc> URL of the page </ loc> </ url>

2. In these blocks you need to define the hreflang information for all variants (including the self-reference)

XML sitemaps can, of course, contain more parameters (for example, *lastmod*, *changefreq*, and *priority*). In the example above, this was omitted in favor of clarity.

Alternative Option #2: HTTP-Header

Alternatively, the hreflang tag can also be located right in the HTTP header (https://support.google.com/webmasters/answer/189077?hl=en).

If you want to provide the hreflang tag via the HTTP header can accomplish this in the following form:

```
Link: <URL1>; rel="alternate"; hreflang="Language 1",<URL2>;
rel="alternate"; hreflang="Language 2"
```

In practice this is what you would get for a German version:

```
Link: <http://www.mywebsite.com/page/>; rel="alternate"; hre-
flang="en",<http://www.mywebsite.com/seite/>; rel="alternate"; hre-
flang="de"
```

Each of the hreflang tags are separated by comma. And, of course, you can include more than just two hreflang tags.

x-default

In addition, there is yet another special hreflang tag that can be used: In the *standard* hreflang tag, either a language or a combination of language and country is used. Instead, you can simply establish what happens with international visitors who may have fallen through the cracks of your traditional hreflang setup by using *x-default*. Let me show you how:

```
<link rel="alternate" hreflang="en"
href="http://www.mywebsite.com/page/" />

<link rel="alternate" hreflang="de"
href="http://www.mywebsite.com/seite/" />

<link rel="alternate" hreflang="x-default"
href="http://www.mywebsite.com/seite/" />
```

The meaning of the first two lines should fairly straightforward by now: English-speaking visitors are sent to the /page/ page, German-speakers to the page /seite/. The only question that remains open is to which page somebody gets sent who does speaks neither German nor English.

And this is precisely where the x-default tag comes into play. Google covers this in the following manner:
(https://webmasters.googleblog.com/2013/04/x-default-hreflang-for-international-pages.html)

"The new x-default hreflang attribute value signals to our algorithms that this page doesn't target any specific language or locale and is the default page when no other page is better suited. For example, it would be the page our algorithms try to show French-speaking searchers worldwide or English-speaking searchers on google.ca.

The same annotation applies for home pages that dynamically alter their contents based on a user's perceived geolocation or the Accept-Language headers. The x-default hreflang value signals to our algorithms that such a page doesn't target a specific language or locale."

Thus, you can specify a *fallback* page with the tag -- a page that can be presented if there is no other logical match via the existing hreflang tag.

Of course it would be ideal not to simply send the users to the German-language home page, as in the example above, but instead to offer them a page where they can select language and/or country manually to match their language needs with appropriate content.

In practice, however, this is often handled differently. Even international websites such as www.salesforce.com in this case simply provide the English-language home page, where you can select the most appropriate language and country at the bottom of the footer.

hreflang and Canonical Tag

Another practical feature of the hreflang tag is the following: Within the hreflang tag Google will find URLs of pages, which are to be presented in the search results -- depending on language and country. At the same time, these pages may have canonical tags. How are they dealt with?

If we choose the following standard example, the pages /page/ and /seite/ are defined in the following manner:

```
<link rel="alternate" hreflang="en"
href="http://www.mywebsite.com/page/" />

<link rel="alternate" hreflang="de"
href="http://www.mywebsite.com/seite/" />
```

Now let's take a look at the canonical tag on these pages. Just a reminder: The canonical tag indicates to Google which is the correct URL (or source) for this page among pages that look the same. The canonical tag is an effective weapon that deals with internal duplicate content, i.e. identical pages on a site that are accessible via multiple URLs.

Let me illustrate this with the following example: You could arrive at the German language page /seite/ via the following URLs:

> http://www.mywebsite.com/seite/

> http://www.mywebsite.com/seite/index.php

> http://www.mywebsite.com/seite/?track=123

In order to signal to Google that these three pages are identical, you would place the same canonical tag on all three pages:

<link rel="canonical" href="http://www.mywebsite.com/seite/"/>

At this point you will probably wonder what would happen if you were to refer to the URL http://www.mywebsite.com/seite/ directly in the hreflang tag where a canonical tag would point to the page http://www.mywebsite.com.com/seite/?track=123. You are basically telling Google: /seite/ is the correct URL (for a German-speaking user), but more precisely: /seite/?track=123.

Unfortunately, the results of the interplay for these parameters (canonical vs. hreflang) isn't clearly defined - and therefore it's safest to completely avoid this problem. I recommend the following best practice: Verify that the URLs defined by the hreflang tag correspond to the canonical tags on their respective pages. Unfortunately, the correctness of the canonical tags cannot be verified by most tools (see next chapter), so you will need to perform a handful of random, manual checks.

6. Verifying the hreflang Tag

On paper all of this looks very feasible. But when actually implementing hreflang tags in the real world, problems always seem to creep up. Sometimes the hreflang tag is missing on certain pages or it points to the wrong page (i.e. all tags point to the home page). Errors like these are relatively tough to isolate manually. You do not have to do this by hand; there are various tools to assist you in verifying the hreflang setup.

Option 1: Check a specific page

One of my top picks for a tool in this case is hreflang.ninja. This tool can be used to check the hreflang tags for a specific page. So if we were to check the home page of Bloofusion Germany, for example, the tool first retrieves the hreflang data from the home page http://www.bloofusion.de/ and then checks all pages that are referred to there. If the hreflang code of www.bloofusion.de (Germany) points to www.bloofusion.at (Austria), then the page http://www.bloofusion.at/ is also checked, because the same codes must be present on that page as well.

hreflang.ninja

See results for http://www.bloofusion.de/ below. Refresh or click here to retest

	hreflang Value	Language	Region	Source	Alternate URL	Errors
✓	de	German	-	html	http://www.bloofusion.de/ ↵	
✓	de-AT	German	Austria	html	http://www.bloofusion.at/ ↵	
✓	de-CH	German	Switzerland	html	http://www.bloofusion.ch/ ↵	
✓	de-DE	German	Germany	html	http://www.bloofusion.de/ ↵	

Illustration 7: Verification of the hreflang tag with the tool hreflang.ninja.

The result of this verification should only contain green check marks in the left column if the hreflang data for this page is correct.

Take note that this tool can be somewhat overzealous and overcritical. Here is a great example from a German retail site to illustrate this: https://www.zalando.de/herrenschuhe/.

The hreflang.ninja tool seems to believe that all hreflang tags are faulty here.

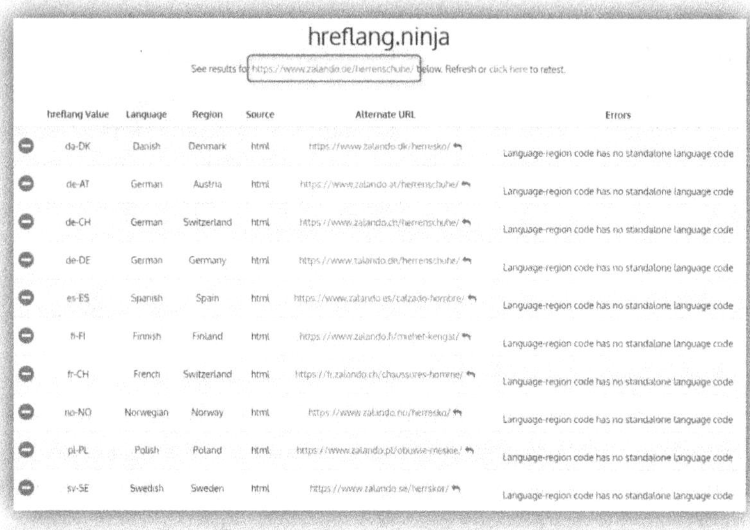

hreflang Value	Language	Region	Source	Alternate URL	Errors
da-DK	Danish	Denmark	html	https://www.zalando.dk/herresko/	Language-region code has no standalone language code
de-AT	German	Austria	html	https://www.zalando.at/herrenschuhe/	Language-region code has no standalone language code
de-CH	German	Switzerland	html	https://www.zalando.ch/herrenschuhe/	Language-region code has no standalone language code
de-DE	German	Germany	html	https://www.zalando.de/herrenschuhe/	Language-region code has no standalone language code
es-ES	Spanish	Spain	html	https://www.zalando.es/calzado-hombre/	Language-region code has no standalone language code
fi-FI	Finnish	Finland	html	https://www.zalando.fi/miehet-kengat/	Language-region code has no standalone language code
fr-CH	French	Switzerland	html	https://fr.zalando.ch/chaussures-homme/	Language-region code has no standalone language code
no-NO	Norwegian	Norway	html	https://www.zalando.no/herresko/	Language-region code has no standalone language code
pl-PL	Polish	Poland	html	https://www.zalando.pl/obuwie-meskie/	Language-region code has no standalone language code
sv-SE	Swedish	Sweden	html	https://www.zalando.se/herrskor/	Language-region code has no standalone language code

Illustration 8: The hreflang.ninja tool complains about Zalando's hreflang tags

What is meant by *Language-region code has no standalone language code*? There are three hreflang tags for de-DE (German language, Germany), de-AT (German language, Austria) and de-CH (German language, Switzerland). With this model German-speaking visitors from Germany, Austria and Switzerland are directed to the appropriate localized sites. But where does a German-speaking searcher end up if she lives in Spain?

According to the tool, there should be an entry that only targets a specific language (i.e. hreflang = "de"). While the hreflang.ninja tool complains about the lack of these entries, Google won't care. At least, it is not considered an error from Google's perspective. In terms of content, however, the hreflang.ninja tool is actually making a correct assessment, since an extended tag would definitely be helpful. Just keep this in mind when using hreflang.ninja.

An alternative tool to hreflang.ninja is the Hreflang Testing Tool by Dejan SEO (http://flang.dejanseo.com.au/). Basically it works similarly but it's not as sensitive. For example, it doesn't complain about the missing language standalone code when it comes to the Zalando site mentioned above.

Illustration 9: The flang Hreflang Testing Tool in action.

Option 2: Check for missing hreflang tags

It's not unusual for hreflang tags to be missing on certain pages of a website. Obviously this would be tough to check manually, so it's best to use a recommended tool here.

For me the Screaming Frog SEO Spider is definitely the tool of choice. With this tool (the full version has a fee, but for fewer than 500 URLs you can use it for free) you can crawl a website and download the results page by page. The first step is to set up the software to check whether the hreflang tag either occurs or doesn't occur on a page. To do this, simply create the following filter entry under *Configuration > Custom > Search*:

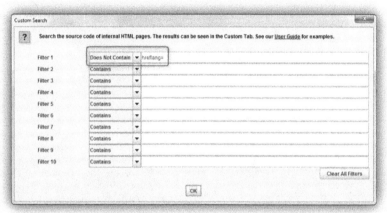

Illustration 10: Set up a search filter that searches for pages without "hreflang."

If you now crawl a website, you can use this filter in the *Custom* tab to determine on which pages the tag is missing. The example of Zalando.de shows that there absolutely are pages missing this tag. In this case, however, this is not an implementation error: some pages are simply not available in the international context, so they do not need the hreflang tag.

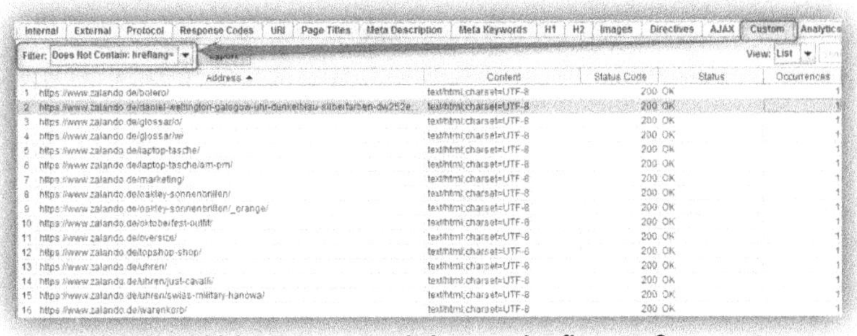

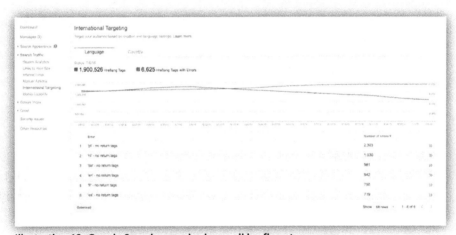

Illustration 11: Which pages currently have no hreflang tag?

Option 3: Incorrect tags across the site

Google Search Console provides yet another way to search for errors. Under the heading *International targeting* you will find in the tab *Language* a listing of the errors found by Google. You can get this report for any property: for all hreflang tags on www.mywebsite.com or for a single directory like www.mywebsite.com/de/.

Illustration 12: Google Search console shows all hreflang tag errors

The report above lists all the pages that contain an hreflang tag and are at the same time missing the so-called return tag.

But let's illustrate this with a specific example. On the http://www.mywebsite.com/seite/ page, there are two hreflang tags to link the English and German-language pages:

```
<link rel="alternate" href="http://www.mywebsite.com/page/" hreflang="en" />
<link rel="alternate" href="http://www.mywebsite.com/seite/" hreflang="de" />
```

The same codes must also be included on the German-language page http://www.mywebsite.com/seite/, so that the hreflang tag can function properly.

But, if the page http://www.mywebsite.com/seite/ only contains the following code, then a return tag is missing:

```
<link rel="alternate" href="http://www.mywebsite.com/seite/" hreflang="de" />
```

Google Search Console will indicate this imbalance with a *no return tags* error message. It means that not all variants of a page contain the complete set of hreflang tags.

To get a list of specific URLs that violate the rule, you simply would click on each respective line. The next step would be to check these URLs step by step with tools like hreflang.ninja.

If you see 100 errors, you do not have to manually deal with 100 URLs. Often, these are systemic errors since the tags may be generated by a system (e-commerce system, content management system, backend programming, etc.).

By the way: In the past, Google Search Console has been known to display errors that were actually not an issue. But once you clicked on and checked the hreflang tags you were informed that all the data was correct.

So you need to take these error messages with a grain of salt. Don't be surprised if errors are displayed which actually not an issue.

Also, don't worry too much about the term *error* since it conjures up visions of a website penalty. This concern is quite unfounded. Worst case is that the hreflang information is not processed. Other adverse effects are currently unknown.

7. Internal Linking and Website Structure

Internal Linking

Google tries to determine which pages of a website are important and which are less important, based on the website structure and especially the internal links. There is an attribute called Link Juice that Google assigns to each page. This Link Juice is distributed via internal links – you could say, it flows through the internal links.

Imagine a simple website. The home page (www.mywebsite.com/) displays a world map and offers three links: the US home page (www.mywebsite.com/us/), the Canadian one (/ca/) and the one for Great Britain (/gb/). Each of these country-specific home pages then link to subpages within the respective section. As a chart it would look like this:

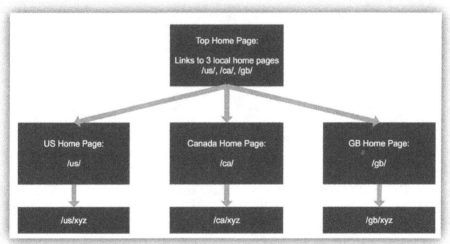

Illustration 13: A typical website structure for a US/Canada/GB site

The way Google actually comes up with an internal linking value isn't 100% clear these days. There used to be the original formula for PageRank, but it has been overtaken by more accurate, less transparent algorithms. Nevertheless, this old and proven model does provide a reasonable basis for our considerations.

With that in mind, let's proceed in the following way:

> The home page has a Link Juice value of 100%.

> This Link Juice proportionally trickles down via internal links.

So if the top home page has 100% Link Juice and links to the three local home pages, then each local home page receives 1/3 of this Link Juice, i.e. 33%.

Graphically this would be represented in the following way:

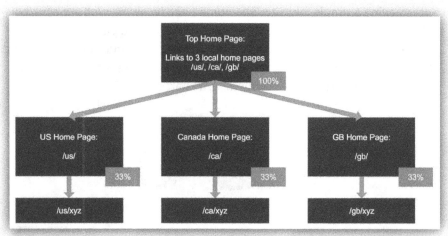

Illustration 14: The distribution of Link Juice across the properties

This kind of distribution would make sense if all countries were of exactly the same importance. In practice, however, this is rarely the case. If, for example, the US accounted for 80% of revenue, it would be silly to give the US home page the same link weight as the Canadian one. The US home page could fare much better with more link energy in a market that is more competitive. The basic rule is that sites with a higher Link Juice value also have a better chance of higher rankings.

Solution #1

The simplest solution is to modify the website structure. If the home page is omitted and you redirect the URL www.mywebsite.com/ to the US homepage via 301 redirect, a completely different picture emerges:

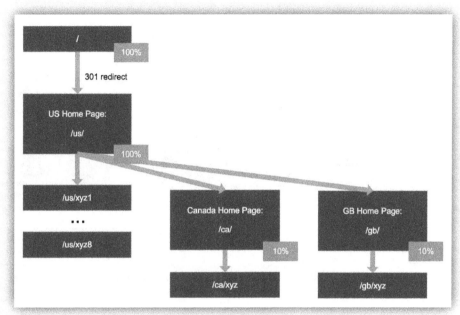

Illustration 15: The US home page receives more Link Juice

Through this 301 redirect, the US home page now receives the entire link power of the parent homepage. How much Link Juice do the Canadian and GB home pages receive? This depends on how many other links are going out from the US page, their source page. In this fictitious example, the US home page links to eight US subpages and additionally to the two local home pages, so that each destination gets one tenth of the original Link Juice, i.e. 10%.

Reality, of course, is much more complicated. But you can see that such a general redirect toward the /us/ home page will shift the link weight strongly in favor of the US section.

Solution #2

So far we have assumed that the US-focused content would reside in a /us/ directory. This doesn't necessarily have to be the case. Often it makes sense not to have the content of the main market in a subdirectory. Then we would only use subdirectories for the other markets -- in this case: /ca/ and /gb/). Here is what that model would look like:

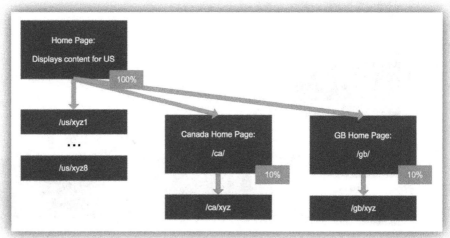

Illustration 16: An alternative structure for the US home page with more Link Juice

The outcome for the internal Link Juice distribution is identical. However, this approach may be viewed as somewhat one-sided: in Solution #1, it is usually easier to separate the different country/language versions in web analytics. In terms of SEO, however, the two solutions are basically equivalent.

Sub-pages

The previous considerations were related to the home page of the website. But what about the sub-pages?

If the number of countries and/or languages to be considered is not too vast, each sub-page of the website should link back to each of the local home pages, so that these home pages each receive their appropriate link energy.

Here is a good example of how you could implement this level of interlinking via a selection menu:

Illustration 17: Selection menu for all countries/languages (Source: www.cargobull.com).

At this point you could easily argue that all countries are receiving the same equivalent link weight, although they probably should not be weighted the same. Another option of attacking this problem more intelligently would be to include only linking to the top five markets and linking the remainder via a selection menu. In our research, however, we have not found an example of this working well. Plus, the sheer simplicity of the selection menu easily justifies the approach above. So, best to keep it simple.

Caution: Automatic Redirects

Some websites also recognize their visitors by their IP address and then automatically redirect them to the appropriate home page. Canadian visitors who access the home page www.mywebsite.com/ would be redirected directly to the local Canadian home page, i.e. the /ca/ page.

This may seem like a good idea for your visitors. However, don't forget that the Googlebot is likely to be redirected as well - and Google's access is likely coming from the US. This may turn into a problem with your international properties since you are also redirecting Google to the English version. Depending on the setup, Google may not even be able to retrieve any foreign language content such as German. (A relatively unlikely event, but we have actually experienced it in a recent project.)

But fear not. To check how your own website is viewed by Google, simply access Google Search Console and select the *Crawl* function *Fetch as Google*. If you type in the home page, you can see under *Status*, if Google can actually reach the home page in question:

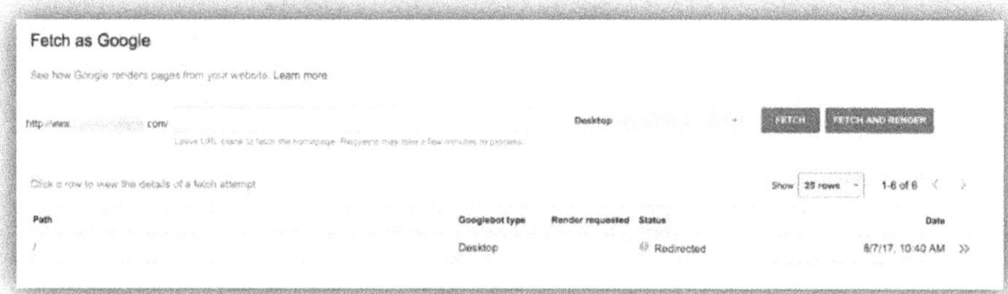

Illustration 18: Verify if Google is redirecting correctly

The status *Redirected* is fairly self-explanatory. When Google reaches this home page, it is immediately redirected to a different page. If you click on *Redirected*, Google Search Console shows which page you are sent to, in this case, the /de/ page:

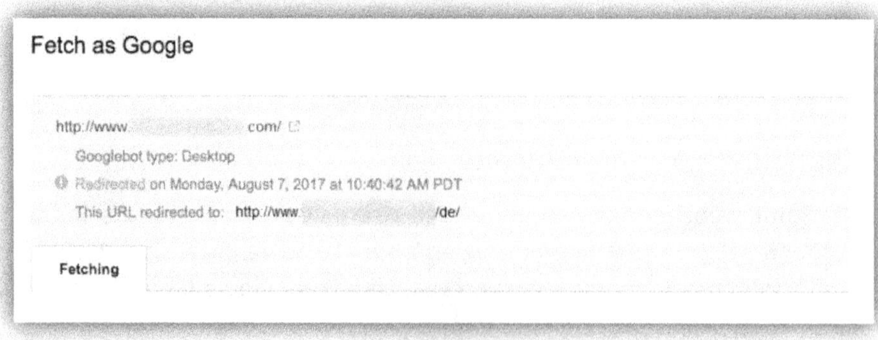

Illustration 19: Verifying the correct redirect to the German site.

In this case everything is as it should be. But it is vital to verify this fact, because redirects like these are not uncommon and extremely difficult to uncover with tools that may be based in other countries.

8. Markup

What is Markup?

Markup can be a relatively complex topic for company individuals who do not deal with HTML every day. If you steer clear of the world of coding, feel free to use this chapter simply to provide your IT staff or design agency with the following recommendations. They will be able to set up your site according to the following two options.

For all others, here we go... Markup is setting up your HTML code to define data semantically. Imagine a site that features details on the two brick-and-mortar locations, typically this would consist of the company name, street address, ZIP code, city, etc. For Google, this is all simple text. Google does not *know* that the text *Santa Cruz* refers to a city in California or that this specific page refers to location information.

Of course, Google could *guess* all this, but that would be precisely that: a simple assumption without backup data. Fortunately, you can insert markers into the HTML code that indicate: This is where the telephone number starts, this is the telephone number, this is where the telephone number ends. In HTML code it could look like this:

```
<div itemscope itemtype="http://schema.org/LocalBusiness">

...

Phone: <span itemprop="telephone">(800) 888-1234</span>

...

</div>
```

The outer <div> element contains the attribute itemtype = "http://schema.org/LocalBusiness", which means that everything within that element contains LocalBusiness data. Within the <div> element, there are different attributes, such as the telephone number, which are framed by the opening <span itemprop = "telephone"> and the closing </ span>.

These markers are ignored by the browser - they do not alter the appearance of the page. But they do help Google recognize this vital information much more effectively.

Schema.org houses a collection of standards for various data types. These standard are called *schema*. A schema defines the different attributes you need to describe an object. There is a *product* schema for product information. Attributes of this schema are price, description and product name.

There are also two interesting examples for local information, which are described in the next section.

Option #1: Organization

One way to provide information about a company is to use the *Organization* Schema. With this schema, you can provide various basic data points, i.e. the name of a company and the logo.

An example of this markup (for complete reference visit http://schema.org/Organization) can be found in the following example. The gray areas must be replaced by the appropriate data:

```
<script type="application/ld+json">
{ "@context" : "http://schema.org",
 "@type" : "Organization",
 "name" : "Name of the organization",
 "url" : "URL of the home page",
 "logo": "URL of a logo",

"address": {
    "@type": "PostalAddress",
    "addressLocality": "City",
    "addressCountry": "US",
    "postalCode": "Zip Code",
    "streetAddress": "Street address"
  },

 "email":"Email address (usually: info@)",
 "telephone":"Phone number",

 "sameAs" : [ "URL of a social media channel",
        "URL of another social media channel",
        "URL of another social media channel" ]
}
</script>
```

Option #2: LocalBusiness (for brick and mortar locations)

The second way of providing local information in a structured way is the LocalBusiness schema (http://schema.org/LocalBusiness). According to Schema.org, it is primarily suitable for local companies:

"A particular physical business or branch of an organization"

Examples for this include a restaurant, a branch of a bank, a bowling alley, etc. Of course, the schema can also be used for each of the individual physical locations of a company.

How to get started? First, you need to know that there are certain subschemas of LocalBusiness that address specific types of local businesses, for example:

> AnimalShelter (http://schema.org/AnimalShelter) = Animal shelters

> AutomotiveBusiness (http://schema.org/AutomotiveBusiness) = Automobile garages and similar companies

> etc.

A complete listing of these schemas can be found at http://schema.org/LocalBusiness. If you are able to locate a suitable template for your company within the list, you should choose that, otherwise simply use the vanilla LocalBusiness schema.

Here is an example of schema feedback by the Google test tool for structured data. You will clearly be able to parse the schema elements, such as type, name, address, etc. as well as any errors or warnings:

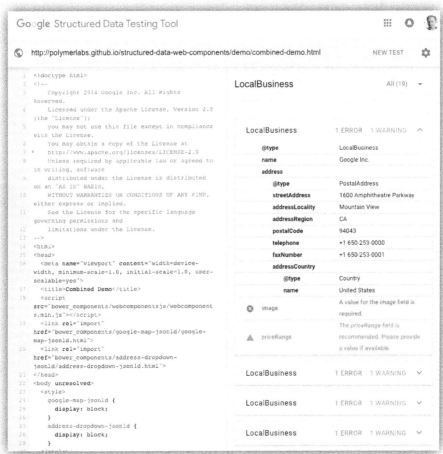

Illustration 20: Markup can be verified via the Google-Test-Tool for Structured Data along with error messages and warnings

As you can see, Google is able to read the information for this location in a structured way (*1 error, 1 warning*). So, if you're using location information on your website, you should take advantage of this schema to provide the best data for Google.

9. Building Local Links

Regardless of whether you opt for one generic domain with country-specific subdirectories or various country-specific domains, don't forget to build your own external inbound links for each country and/or language version.

Here is a concrete example: According to our link database, there are a total of about 300 external websites which link to www.datastax.com - leaders in data management in cloud applications. The company also has different language websites, such as www.datastax.de (German) and www.datastax.fr (French). The German home page, www.datastax.de, has very few inbound links from other German sites. Local links from Germany would be instrumental for the German site to receive more link energy and thus better rankings.

In principle, two different approaches should be considered for link building:

1. Your own website already has external links, but these are pointing to the wrong site. For example: A well-known German high tech news site, https://www.heise.de links to the US home page https://www.datastax.com/, but not actually to the more appropriate German country home page, https://www.datastax.de. In this case the links should be changed by contacting the website in question. You would then provide them the better link and consider steps needed to be taken in the future that this doesn't happen again.

2. Your own website does not have any international inbound links at all. In this case, steps should be taken to create a link strategy and start building such links.

These two approaches will be discussed in more detail below.

Case #1: Inbound Links Are Pointing to the Incorrect Page or Website

To verify who is linking to your site, especially if it is to the wrong page, you can use a database like ahrefs.com or majestic.com. Now you can download all external links for a website in question.

With the ahrefs tool you also have the option of downloading similar links. This means you work with unique links only and can truly dig into the analysis. In this case it is the difference between analyzing 8,443,346 rows of links versus 30,814. A convenient time-saving feature.

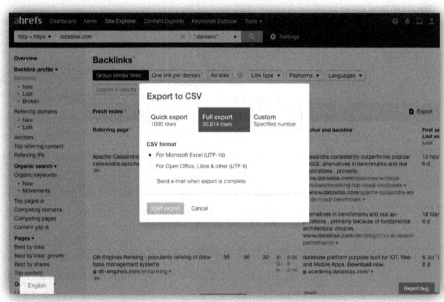

Illustration 21: Exporting all inbound links for the domain datastax.com

Once you have the link data in an Excel spreadsheet in front of you, you can now easily filter these. The columns of interest are: *Referring Page* (from this external page) and *Link URL* (to this internal page). Now you can verify all links manually or, much better, set up a filter. If you use *Data -> Filter* within Excel to sort the Referring Page column by *contains .de/*, you quickly get links from all .de domains. But this is not very fun.

The ultimate ninja approach is to take advantage of one of the brand-new features within the ahrefs tool – the backlink filter. Not only can you filter by link type, (dofollows, redirects, governmental, educational, etc.) and by platforms (blogs, ecommerce, message boards, etc.) but also by language.

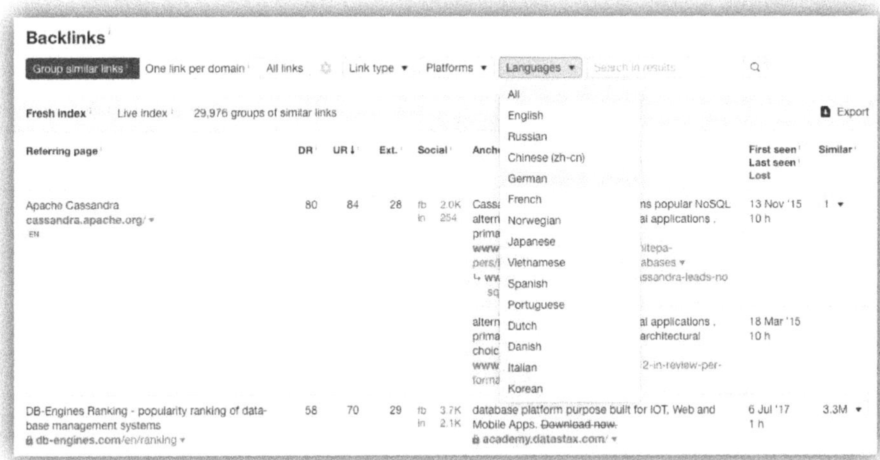

Illustration 22: Using the ahrefs tool to filter out country-specific backlinks

This would make it a snap to analyze the German backlinks and determine which ones link to the US section instead of the German section of the site.

Once this project is completed, the work isn't quite done yet. You still have to monitor any new links that appear from this point on. This can also be covered fairly easily with the ahref tool. You can set a date and immediately track any new backlinks within that timeframe. Even better: you can set up alerts that will conveniently remind you once a month.

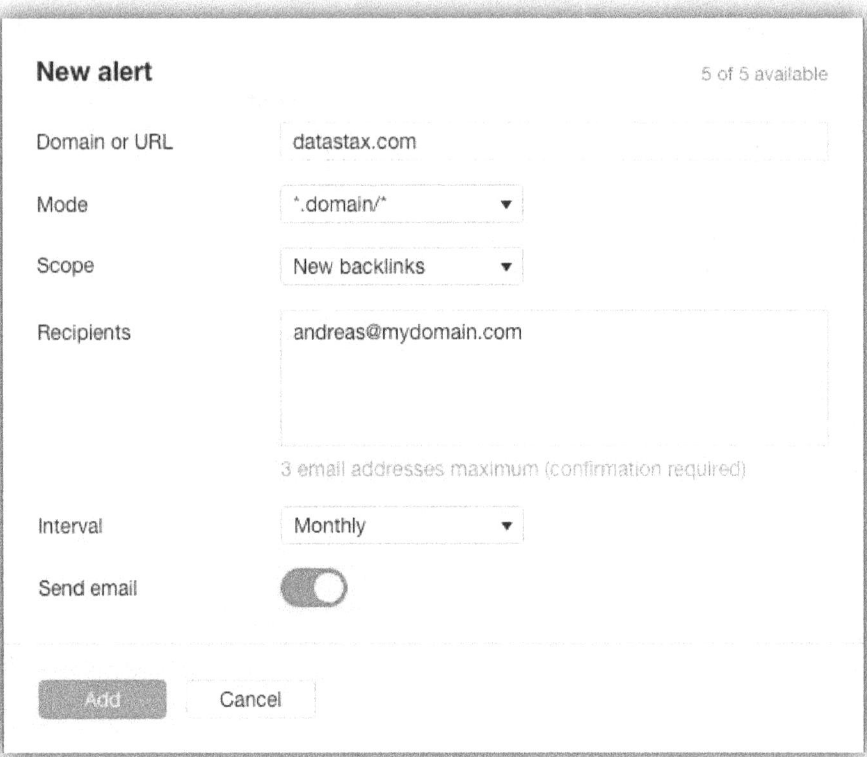

New alert

Domain or URL	datastax.com
Mode	*.domain/* ▼
Scope	New backlinks ▼
Recipients	andreas@mydomain.com

3 email addresses maximum (confirmation required)

Interval	Monthly ▼
Send email	⬤

Add   Cancel

Illustration 23: Ahrefs alerts to monitor new backlinks that need to be verified.

In this case you should be aware that *new* doesn't necessarily mean that the link is genuinely new. It simply is considered new for ahrefs, meaning that it hasn't been spotted before. At the end of the day, you are still periodically unearthing links that should be dealt with either by updating them if they still make sense but don't point to the best page or by having them deleted if they are out of date.

And there is nobody out there who likes an up-to-date site more than Google.

Case #2: Targeted Link Building

In addition to the previous steps you should be focused on building local links yourself. As a rule this task is much more easily dealt with by following a targeted and structured approach.

Typically you would start things out with an audit of already existing links to derive a strategy for local link building. As a rule, there usually are good amounts of backlinks that have been created organically. This proves to all of us that there are solid reasons for external sites to be interested and willing to link back to your site. By far the best motivation for external links is if you feature truly compelling and unique content that is virtually begging to be linked to.

Here is an example: Imagine the site http://www.agricultural-machinery.com. It that already has various high-quality links from US distributors, i.e. http://www.us-agri-distributor-A.com and http://www.us-agri-distributor-B.com. The next logical step would be to contact the French distributors and have them link to the appropriate French section of the site: http://www.agricultural-machinery.com/fr. A friendly, custom email indicating that other distributors are all linking to the site often will be sufficient. Mentioning that other distributors already are linking to the site will often increase motivation and accelerate the process.

Playing by the Rules

Anyone involved in building links can potentially get in trouble with the Google guidelines. If you violate these rules, your site could fall victim to a Google penalty. Obviously, this must be avoided since it ultimately has a negative effect on your rankings and thus your traffic.

Google provides a good overview of the most important cornerstones on this guideline: https://support.google.com/webmasters/answer/66356 page. Basically, the entire topic is complex because many definitions are in a gray area. And unfortunately there is no instance that clearly states which link is acceptable and which violates the guidelines.

The following list, therefore, does not claim to be complete, but certainly covers the most important cases. Each company should examine the directives outlined here and, in the case of uncertainty, refrain from an implementation.

Buying links is definitely against the guidelines - unless the purchase is not primarily related to the link. If you get registered in a high-quality industry directory for a fee, the link is often considered a byproduct. If the main reason for your motivation here is for your company to appear in a print/digital directory because of access to potential clients, then the link us usually not objectionable, because the fee was not paid specifically for the link.

If you were to remunerate a blog owner for a link and really only acquire this link to influence Google, the link clearly violates the guidelines.

By the same token this is true, if **product samples** are in play, even if no money has been exchanged. If you, the owner of an ecommerce site, were to offer free product samples for testing and, and as a result, a link is created, then this violates the guidelines, because the primary goal of the action was the link. If, however, you feature a raffle and the winner is then linked to your website, then this link is not objectionable, assuming that the raffle was not primarily created as link bait.

Link exchanges should be viewed with a critical eye. If website A links to B and B then links back to A this means there is a link exchange. If these activities are kept to a reasonable and natural level, then Google shouldn't have too much of a problem. But if a large number of exchanged links surface, then this can become critical.

Guest post linking is also not without its risks. Anyone who publishes a single post on an industry portal and, in return, receives a link at the end of the post in the about-the-author's box. No concerns. However, if you outsource guest posts on a large scale, and often link them directly from within the post, this could cause problems with the guidelines.

At the end of the day, the goal of all activities here is for the so-called **link profile** (i.e. the totality of all links) to look **organic**. All links should pass the **Smell Check**: Does a website visitor who looks at a link believe that this link comes from a *real* website that represents added value for its users? And does the visitor assume that the link is natural, i.e. created without any time or money invested?

Again: The difference between good and bad links is very much in flux and difficult to nail down, even by SEO professionals. Thus, only bet on link strategies that stay away from violating any guidelines. They are there for a reason.

10. Google Search Console: Settings

Setting up Properties

As already mentioned, you can create as many properties as you like in Google Search Console (previously known as Google Webmaster Tools). So if you decide to implement sub-directories for your international content, you can set up a property not only for the complete website www.mywebsite.com, but also for the individual international directories such as www.mywebsite.com/de/, www.mywebsite.com/fr/ and so on. If, on the other hand, you use subdomains, you can also design them as properties (for example, de.mywebsite.com, fr.mywebsite.com).

In any case, it is vital to understand that the protocol belongs to a property. So you can create a property for http://www.mywebsite.com and a separate one for the secure site https://www.mywebsite.com. You would then also receive different data for the properties, depending on whether the HTTP or HTTPS results are in play.

With secure vs. non-secure sites it is clearly recommended to make a choice of which variant is best (i.e., HTTPS) and the other version (i.e. HTTP) then to redirect to it via 301-redirect so that only one protocol can be found in the search results.

Let's assume that a site wants to use the HTTPS protocol and uses the directory model for the language variants on the site. (Analogously, this approach works for subdomains as well.) First, you have to set up the domain itself as a property. Simply log into Google Search Console and select *Add a Property*:

Illustration 24: Adding a new HTTPS Site as a property

Now you also have to make sure to add all appropriate international directories as properties, i.e.:

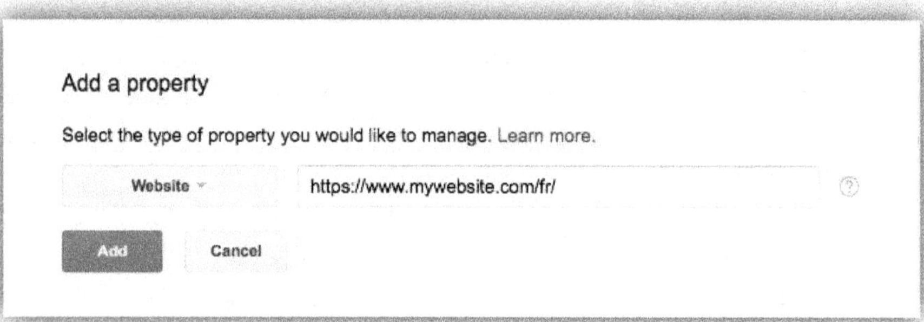

Add a property

Select the type of property you would like to manage. Learn more.

| Website ▾ | https://www.mywebsite.com/fr/ | ⑦ |

Add   Cancel

Illustration 25: Adding language directories as a property

International Targeting

Once this is done, Google Search Console can be used to target the different properties to the appropriate countries. Unfortunately, it isn't possible to target a property to a language, although this would be a useful feature.

Also, be aware that that targeting works only for generic domains. You can't take the country-specific domain www.mywebsite.de and *renationalize* to another country. With a generic domain (.com, .info, .net, etc.) this is not an issue.

Targeting a country is a relatively straightforward process. Just select *International Targeting* and the *Country* tab. I.e.:

Illustration 26: A property being mapped to a specific country via international targeting

Consider the consequences of these international setting – which can be changed at any time, by the way. If you set up a French-speaking section (/fr/) and target it to France, then that section will have good rankings in that geographical area. Outside of France this section of your site will have sub-average rankings because Google always shows a preference to local results in for local searches.

You would typically only target properties to a specific country if the property **primarily serves that country**. Here is an example: If the Spanish-speaking section of a website should directed primarily to the inhabitants of Spain and no other Spanish-speaking countries (particularly in South America), this property should be set up for Spain and only Spain.

Targeting is ideally integrated into the planning stages of a web site. So if you are battling with the decision whether to create directories or subdomains for specific languages or for specific countries, you might want to decide in favor of countries. Because then Google Search Console can be conveniently used to map the individual country properties to the right countries.

Setting up Access Rights

The use of country and language-specific properties has a further advantage: All properties can be created centrally in order to give the local staff in the respective countries access to the relevant data only.

Under the menu item *Settings* there is the option *Users and Property Owners*. This is where the central administrator can set up users (*Add A New User*) either with restricted or full access. *Restricted* simply means that although you cannot make any changes to the settings, you have full access the search analysis data.

You thus have the flexibility to specify which functions the individual *local staff* is allowed to access. If you want to avoid giving these local team members the ability to muddle sensitive settings, simply stick with *restricted* access for them.

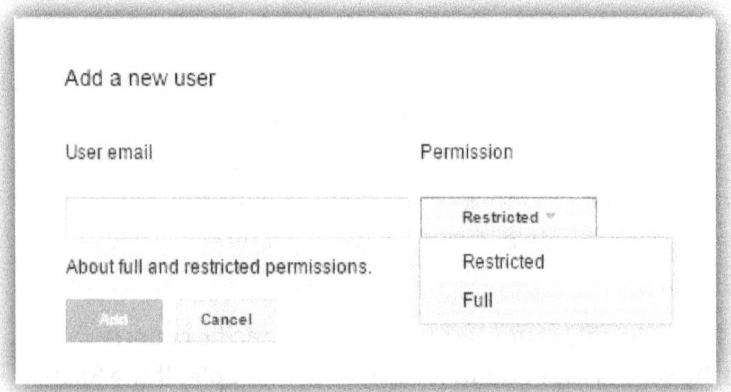

Illustration 27: Add additional users to Google Search Console

Managing Sets

New in Google Search Console is the feature allowing you to merge multiple properties into a single *virtual* property. One can therefore combine the individual properties that have been created for countries and languages into a so-called *set*.

For a set like this you can then collectively unite country and language data that logically belongs together. Some examples could be D/A/CH (Germany/Austria/Switzerland) or EMEA. This will group the properties according to your target regions and can be a very helpful feature to slice data.

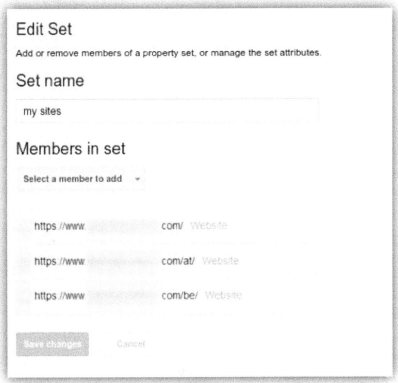

Illustration 28: Via the sets functionality you can easily summarize properties

It is interesting to note that all the data that can be retrieved for a domain from Google Search Console can also be accessed for each prop-erty. So, if you have created a country/language-specific property, you can easily view the indexed pages for that specific property under *Index Status*. If you have already set up the subdirectories /fr/ and /es/ within Search Console, you can quickly see how many pages Google has indexed from these local directories.

Illustration 29: Ability to check the Index Status for each property

In any case, it is strongly recommenced to provide a separate XML-Sitemap for each country or language. This has the advantage to clearly iden-tify how many pages Google has indexed in Google Search Console. Under the menu option *Sitemaps* you can then see what data was submitted under *Submitted* (listed in the XML Sitemap) and *Indexed* (included in the index by Google). This makes it much easier to see if there are indexing problems for certain languages or countries.

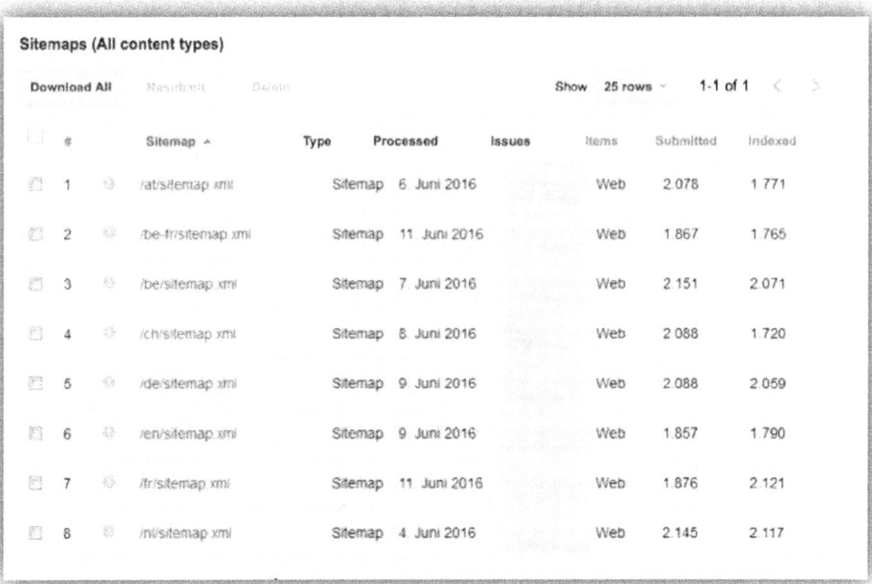

Sitemaps (All content types)

	#		Sitemap ▲	Type	Processed	Issues	Items	Submitted	Indexed
	1		/at/sitemap.xml	Sitemap	6. Juni 2016		Web	2.078	1.771
	2		/be-fr/sitemap.xml	Sitemap	11. Juni 2016		Web	1.867	1.765
	3		/be/sitemap.xml	Sitemap	7. Juni 2016		Web	2.151	2.071
	4		/ch/sitemap.xml	Sitemap	8. Juni 2016		Web	2.088	1.720
	5		/de/sitemap.xml	Sitemap	9. Juni 2016		Web	2.088	2.059
	6		/en/sitemap.xml	Sitemap	9. Juni 2016		Web	1.857	1.790
	7		/fr/sitemap.xml	Sitemap	11. Juni 2016		Web	1.876	2.121
	8		/nl/sitemap.xml	Sitemap	4. Juni 2016		Web	2.145	2.117

Download All   Resubmit   Delete   Show   25 rows ▾   1-1 of 1   ‹ ›

Illustration 30: One sitemap should be added for every country/language

11. Additional Diagnostic Tools

Google Search

Search results are always localized on the basis of language and country. In other words, a Google.de (Google Germany) user will primarily be presented German-language content from Germany, while a Google.at (Google Austria) user will mostly see German-language content from Austrian sites.

Here's a convenient way to verify which websites or web pages are found in the respective country or language version of Google: Simply verify your query via the local version of Google, i.e. www.google.at (for Austria) or www.google.fr (for France). In countries where there are more than one languages (i.e. Canada, Belgium or Switzerland), this language choice option is offered directly on the Google home page. Thus you may be offered the Swiss Google homepage in German when visiting Google.ch. However, you can easily switch to other the other appropriate local languages:

Illustration 31: Visitors see each of the language choices applicable to their location

Another way to get localized results is to use Google's Advanced Search functionality, which can be accessed via https://www.google.com/advanced_search. On this page you can set various options. Most practical to you will be to select language and country explicitly. Here we use an example query for the B2B firm "IBM" to demonstrate its usefulness. Thus you can check how the search results would look for *Dutch* (language) in *Belgium* (country):

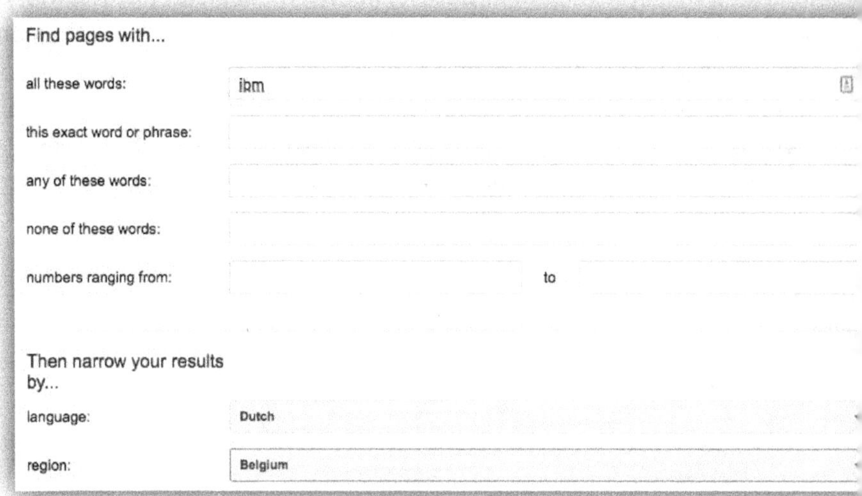

Find pages with...	
all these words:	ibm
this exact word or phrase:	
any of these words:	
none of these words:	
numbers ranging from:	to

Then narrow your results by...	
language:	Dutch
region:	Belgium

Illustration 32: Via Advanced Search you can individually select language/region

This yields the following result:

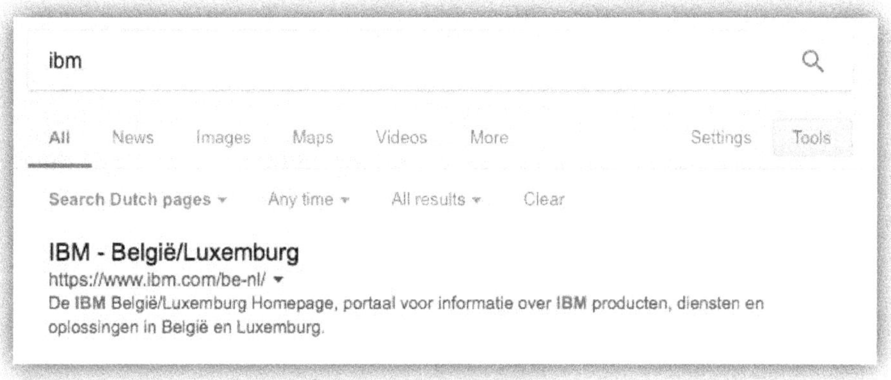

Illustration 33: A search result for the Dutch language...

By changing the option to "French" (Language) in Advanced Search for Belgium, you will see very different results. And they are as expected:

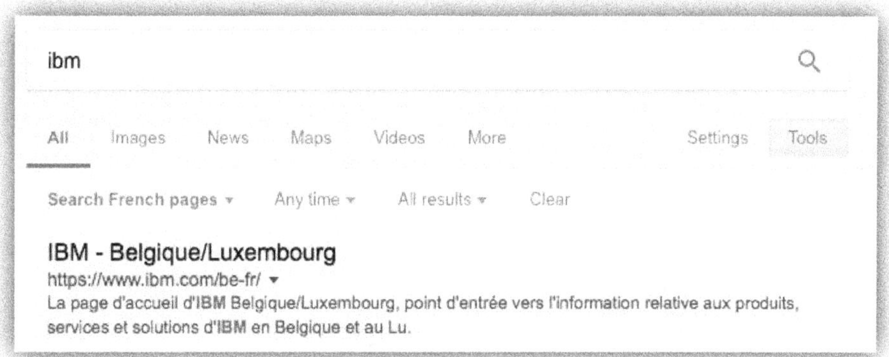

Illustration 34: ... and for the French language

You can clearly see that depending on the language selected, the user will get different search results for the same website within the same country. The advanced search lets you verify which search results are preferred by Google for a specific combination of country and language. Just be aware that there can be minor differences between what the local Google search engine (google.be) delivers versus what the Advanced Search tool shows you.

All in all, the query via the local Google search page is probably closer to the actual results than the Advanced Search tool. But since these days there isn't just *one true search result* this isn't a drawback. You have to take into consideration that every search result you are provided is localized and personalized by the Google algorithm.

But both approaches will help by indicating if Google is showing the right results for the correct website page. The example with the *IBM* search illustrates that if you have created content in the languages Dutch and French for the country Belgium then a search with the appropriate language/region parameters should yield the correct language/region results.

Google Search Console

To check whether the correct website or section is delivered for a particular country in the search results, you can also use Google Search Console. There is the function *Search Analytics*, which gives you an insight into your organic visits such as:

- Which search queries have been entered?

- How often were certain listings displayed ("Impressions") and then clicked on ("Clicks" and "Click Through Rate")?

First, you should set the maximum time span to maximize data quality -- currently it is limited to 90 days. Google has promised to provide more data here, but this is feature still being worked on.

If you select *Countries* and then *Filter Countries* then all countries for which a particular site has received visits are displayed. The following is a .com domain. You can tell that this domain receives visitors from India, the UK, Canada and some other countries:

Illustration 35: In which countries was the website dispayed and clicked on?

Let's say you had a Canadian web site (.ca) dedicated to traffic from Canada. The hreflang tag was implemented so that visitors from Canada would land on the .ca domain, whereas visitors from the UK would be directed to the .co.uk domain. By using this Search Analytics function you would expect visitors from the UK and the US to be absent when checking the .ca domain. If not, you would need to verify the set up of your hreflang tags for your Canadian site.

With Google Search Console, you can easily check whether a website for a specific country shows up in the right search results or not. To use a European example: If you had a .de (German), a .at (Austrian) and a .ch (Swiss) domain and linked them correctly via the appropriate hreflang tags, then Google Search Console should funnel visitors from the three target countries, Germany, Austria, and Switzerland to the correct local websites.

Final Thoughts

Hopefully this book has helped you develop some guidelines that will aid you in making the following decisions more efficiently:

> What should my international domain strategy look like?

> How do I take advantage of hreflang tags so the right international audience sees the appropriate content?

> How can I use tools, especially Google Search Console, to get things set up correctly and verify all of the steps involved?

Of all of the ideas presented, this one stands at the very top: Your approach needs to be focused and strategic. I firmly believe that especially the choice of your domain strategy will be one of your most important decisions. A deliberate decision that you should take time making. This choice represents a long-term direction that the entire company needs to ultimately stand behind.

Now the good news: None of this is rocket science. Most of these recommendations don't get put into action because of lack of knowledge. But since you now are part of the enlightened crowd, it's time to roll up your sleeves and implement some of this goodness.

At the end of the day, if you still have a need for feedback or additional consultation dealing with international SEO, please get in touch with Bloofusion. I'm happy to receive any input (seobook@bloofusion.com). Feel free to connect via Linkedin as well (https://www.linkedin.com/in/searchenginemarketing/).

See you soon!

Andreas & Markus

About the Authors

Andreas Mueller and Markus Hoevener are the co-founders of Bloofusion, a digital growth agency focused on making websites do what they were designed to do: Generate leads and sales instead of just looking pretty. We are located in Santa Cruz, California (www.bloofusion.com) as well as Emsdetten, Germany (www.bloofusion.de) where we serve the North American as well as the German, Austrian and Swiss markets.

Both Markus and Andreas are active in the digital marketing industry. Publishing blogs, articles and their German monthly search magazine, they also present frequently at online conferences around the world.

What brought them together initially on that fateful day in 2002? At the time, Markus had his finger on the technical pulse of the times having just coded one of Europe's first search engines and Andreas intimately understood the needs of a VP of Marketing, having been in that role for two software firms since 1993. Putting their techie and marketing brains together, they founded Bloofusion and have never looked back.

Markus's favorite quote summarizes our combined approach well:

Life is great. The rest is just details.